The Assumption

The
Assumption

Bryan D. Dietrich

WORDFARM
SEATTLE, WASHINGTON

WordFarm
2816 E. Spring St.
Seattle, WA 98122
www.wordfarm.net
info@wordfarm.net

Cover Image: iStockphoto
Cover Design: Andrew Craft

USA ISBN-13: 978-1-60226-008-5
USA ISBN-10: 1-60226-008-7
Printed in the United States of America
First Edition: 2011

Library of Congress Cataloging-in-Publication Data

Dietrich, Bryan D.
The assumption : poems / Bryan D. Dietrich. -- 1st ed.
   p. cm.
ISBN 978-1-60226-008-5 (pbk.)
I. Title.
PS3604.I37A88 2011
811'.6--dc22

        2011016226

P 10 9 8 7 6 5 4 3 2 1
Y 16 15 14 13 12 11

Acknowledgments

I would like to thank those venues in which the following poems have appeared:

Isotope	"The Engineer"
American Literary Review	"The Skeptic"
Nimrod	"The Crackpot"
Campbell Corner (Sarah Lawrence College)	"The Astronomer"
Paris Review	"The Magician"
Western Humanities Review	"The Writer"
Bellingham Review	"The Believer"
X-Connect	"The Heat Death of the Universe"

Thanks also to *Isotope* for awarding "The Engineer" its Editors' Prize for 2007. And to U.S. Spaceways for allowing the second of these particular sonnets to travel with Scotty into space that same year.

Finally, thanks to the mad assumptions of all the poets, particularly the daemonic ones, and to the many speculative writers whose works first transported me to other worlds: Atwood, Barker, Bellairs, Borges, Bradbury, Burroughs, Byrne, Camus, Carter, Clarke, Crowley, Delany, Donaldson, Ellison, Faulkner, Gaiman, Gibson, Gilman, Hawthorne, Heinlein, Jackson, Kafka, King, Kirby, Kubrick, Lee, L'Engle, Le Guin, Leiber, Lessing, Lovecraft, Du Maurier, McKillip, Miller, Moench, Moore, Morrison, Oates, O'Connor, Orwell, Poe, Rice, Roddenberry, Rushdie, Shelley, Sturgeon, Tolkien, Turner, Twain, Verne, Vonnegut, and Wells.

for Will Orr & Carl Sagan
one believer, one skeptic

Contents

It's wanting to know that makes us matter.

—Tom Stoppard

THE ENGINEER

What are our learned men save the descendants
of witches and hermits who crouched in caves
and in woods brewing herbs, interrogating shrewmice
and writing down the language of the stars?

—Virginia Woolf

The Engineer

—In Memory of James Doohan

I.

Between the dust clouds calving sun to night,
behind the blazing battlements of old
auroral habiliments, dead supernova's light,
surrounded by these gases growing gold,
we wander. From cloud to cloud of matter
clutter, where holy cauldrons spin, sputter,
where chaos reigns and, under thunder, worlds
congeal beneath the peal of heaven plunder—

meteorites, lightning strikes—from whole herds
of icy shards shepherded by stellar sway
to planets, less than paradise, where crust gives way
to crack, crater, ponds of stagnant wonder
we trek. Energy, synergy, blind erection.
This manic, inorganic, immaculate conception.

II.

This. Manic, organic, immaculate,
our conception, our long lust for cause,
this need, perhaps greed, for eternal laws
sends us, spores, Earth's whores, ejaculate,
back to the abyss, the whence we commenced,
back to tomb, womb, cosmic amniotic sac.
Here, death's foes (little Prosperos, Poe's), dance
the dance of red to black. Like orphans we lack,

hunger for first embrace, to retrace the race.
In all we do, we echo the urge to crave
some sun, what fills—from crater to pond to cave,
from Plato to Pluto, Dido to Odo—space.
The dark is more than only, lonely, full of fear.
It's made us seek, as Stevens said, an Engineer.

III.

In seeking, as Stevens said, an Engineer—
whether Sunday morning, porch turned church,
looking back on pagan feast, that need to lurch
forward, past winter, past night where night's veneer
suggests nothing more than nothing beneath,
no prop, no crop, only the end, with teeth—
in search of another sun to unswallow the old,
to end anxiety, absence, an eternity of cold,

in hope the babe would come, steal back his scythe,
provide solution through ablution, at last arrive. . . .
In believing, deeming—Sun to Son, Sol to soul—
that seeking fire was more than this, a Titan's toll,
more than matter needing matter, well, we swore
to boldly go where none had gone before.

IV.

So we go, boldly, back where we came before,
go blindly, proudly, in ships of steel, sterling ore,
go, go returning, past time itself, the core,
cavity, gravity, what drove us to this shore.
Matter driving matter to the heart of matter:
loss. Even Pound, poet, mad as a hatter,
knew the rest was dross. So we scatter
in these ships, these grails, each endless platter

a helping of us. And we reach, we send up flares,
catching something of the stars we seek, angels, unaware.
We push through all that emptiness, each portal, each tear,
knowing that we seek the end, what isn't there,
ships becoming stars themselves, something adorning
nothing. First star to the right and straight on 'til morning.

V.

First star to the right? Straight on until?
What could this mean but that we're lost,
awaiting reentry, standing on the sill?
Peter pecking shadow, Wendy tempest tossed.
We want for Father, shadow. Even Hook
would do. Some captain, any Captain,
the one Whitman cried for between
astronomer and star, star and star's journeywork.

Walt died seeking sacred hieroglyph,
but isn't that all we are, our substance
spun out—spider sputum, maker myth—
across each rhizome horizon called chance?
Bracing nascence against darkness, we clap, we fly.
Freud fingered this fire, our bellies, called it Y.

VI.

Freud, fingers, fire belly. Captain, father,
why. Chromosome or Chronos, we linger,
hunger, die. War's the same. And lust and nuns.
We need an answer to oppose itch, these thumbs.
Event horizon, Kuiper belt, Apollo 11,
Juno Beach. . . . We stand by cusp, by bier,
looking for something to stoke our heaven,
for someone to answer fire with fire.

Hate or love, we ask for passage, officer,
doctor, crew, for something more than empty hull,
for everything, anything *beyond* the pull,
to give it reason. Klingon, Sargon, Lucifer.
Any con will do. Any origin, passion, play.
Not parents of stone, gas alone, recombinant DNA.

VII.

Our parents? Cold stone. Hot gas. A little DNA.
Where the gods, goddesses, some holy sobriquet?
Pater, Madre, Engineer, Intelligent Design?
Where Prime Directive? Beneficent, malign?
We do not wish to see ourselves as beast-bred, aping tools,
though no one has a problem being kin to molecules.
So take in hand, one, chemistry, and two, a teeming brain.
Mix in dreams of Eden in an interstellar rain.

Dilithium and nacelles we'll need. Perhaps a shuttlecraft.
But none of this can work without a soul to man the raft.
We've needed one, an Engineer, to make us, take us up.
Our fear is what has brought us here, oh Captain. Breaking up.
Yes, fears are what have brought us here, captains of the night,
sons of suns, engineers, dust clouds calving light.

THE ASSUMPTION:
A CROWN OF CROWNS

It might be so—but the time is not yet.
Speed it, O Father! Let thy Kingdom come!

—Samuel Taylor Coleridge

The Skeptic

If you tasted it, it would first taste bitter,
then briny, then surely burn your tongue.
It is like what we imagine knowledge to be . . .

—Elizabeth Bishop

I.

The assumption is it hasn't happened
yet. There are those, of course, who claim communion
with the odd, with emanations, vow reunion
in the sky. Once, twice, they say, night opened
its else to them, let logic spill through. Upend
their rhetoric, though, begin with the onion
and, even trusting a rusted blade, religion
always greets you, skinless in the end.

It isn't that I don't believe in little
grey men. Trust me, intelligence is out
there. But why here? Why now? Why Fiddle
Creek, Iowa? There are signs, always, we should doubt:
no ship parts, no star charts. Just rumors of metal
fragments. Commandments. A fire. A mount.

II.

Fragments, commandments, a fire, a mount
of flying green olives. I don't know what
they expect, the believers. When one gets caught
in a lie, tossing, say, his favorite rock
into a sky full of nothing but that
which people want to see, the head count
only doubles, the shutters click shut, and we
turn to cover up, to gators in the sewer.

Take the woman who lives on my block;
her gout got better touring Bermuda.
Now she climbs her roof every night, chock
full of hope, hubris, not a little Kahlúa,
and strips herself to the stars. She says *they* see.
I say the only ones who watch are grackles, the Hubble, me.

III.

I say the only ones to watch are grackles.
The Hubble and me, well, we see eye
to eye; if we catch some saucer in the act, less
mystery, yes, but why go looking? The fact is,
no astronomer with two good mirrors
to rub together has spotted squat. Sure, errors
have been made—the occasional spy
plane off course; that astronaut whose hackles

harried him into misreading backwash
from his own craft; a few blips here, there, or
even those geese mistaken for alien fly
by—but always, it's the same. The lie
is not the consort of conspiracy,
it's ours. We woo it, as we must our terrors.

IV.

It's ours. We woo it as we must. Our terror
(wrought as though from prophecy, from lack
of understanding, from a fear of other
silences less lonely than our own) grows black
and blasted in every wasteland, every era,
owing no allegiance to the tack
taken by just, say, modernity. The situations,
administrations, names of singular stretches

of sod may evolve, revolve, but the sketches
in our caves remain. Bear becomes fear,
fear, famine, famine a god who catches
us when we fall. We deify implications—
hemorrhagic fever, cattle mutilations—
making disease design, prophet, profiteer.

V.

Making disease, design, prophet, profiteer,
the network of our own devising—
the media if you must—trots them out
every so often for air, time, a little season.
Shakers, Quakers, those who've long lapped their reason
cavalcade before us. They do not hear
God, but voices of Regulus rising
from implants in the rear. Though I doubt

they've seen the hindquarters of the holy
of holies, many claim messengers
came, collected their ovaries, prodded
their posteriors with pipe. Others were coddled,
bottled it's said, shipped home less injuries
to those who can't distinguish hoax from homily.

VI.

To those who can't distinguish hoax from homily,
who pray for *their* return across the Galilee,
who seem to need more leg room than mere Galaxy
in which to stretch out awe, Mars, apparently,
needs women. Sure. And Sodom its idolatry.
But there, too, are those who would summarily
dismiss large wooden horses, the gates of Troy.
The difference is *believers* lack respect

for what even Peter knew sinking in the sea,
troubled, the color of his own doubt. They don't suspect
(regardless of a dearth of honest mystery
gone fallow in a fine fuddle of forget)
nothing quite appalls, enthralls like entropy.
Sin perhaps. Imaginary Magi with a net.

VII.

Sin perhaps. . . . Emergent Magi. . . . Indra's net. . . .
Olfactory application of the vomeronasal
organ. . . . The sociopath *cum* hemosexual
god who sold his soul to Imhotep. . . .
Crop circles cut into corn like crude relief maps
of hell. . . . Somewhere in the intellectual
Mecca of the midwest, a hanger, damn normal,
save for seven tiny bodies, Handiwrapped. . . .

Doesn't matter which (Halley's, Shoemaker, Kohoutek,
pink pills for comet fever), the shills jonesing
for a sign that, Einstein notwithstanding,
God *does* play dice, will find one. Still, I'd bet
the farm, all of Roswell, even Nazca's "landing"
lines, whatever the assumption is, it hasn't happened yet.

The Crackpot

*I will put up with any mockery rather than pretend
that I am satisfied when I am hungry. I know,
anyway, that I will not be put off with a compromise,
with a recurring zero, simply because it is consistent
with the laws of nature and actually exists.*

—Fyodor Dostoevsky

I.

There are those, of course, who claim communion
is a crock, that contact, the new dispensation
from a sky packed to incandescence
with friendly alien fire, is luminescence
only, bad manna, false host hung from the tongue
of a people grown gaunt with thirst and exile. Jung
might've called it collective recollection, Apollo
fixation, synaptic aberration. Mandala.

It's not that. See, I don't believe in belittling
the large with largesse. No, the unsettling
gospel is simpler, more or less. Prevailing
sentiment would have it that the wailing
wall is localized phenomena, a place.
But Earth is *all* Jerusalem, viewing it from space.

II.

Earth is all Jerusalem. Viewing it from space,
though, this race must seem futile, faint, bent
on beating Jacob to the punch. They *have* sent
emissaries, you know, the commonplace
ball of fire, even wheels within wheels within clear
sky showers. Yet each time the atmosphere
beetles high above us, cracking open carapace
for wings, we opt only to dissect, to lay waste

the chariots and name them, simply, solar flares.
Religion, academe, the government. . . .
None want us reading universal prayers
left at the foot of the wall, this Earth, its nearby stairs,
stars so ladder-like we seem about to mount.
We wrestle, not gods, but ghosts of gods we fear to count.

III.

We wrestle, not gods, but ghosts of gods. We fear
to count them in, dare not count them out,
refuse the peroration of their presence here—
that blink in a crowd threatening nictitation—deny
their greater romantic equations, stellar Ameslan
nonlinear and holy, writ high in the sky.
Once, it was not madness to look up, shout
God, cry succubus, negotiate with Nephilim,

secure doors and daughters against their certain
coming. The giants in the Earth those days were Talls
mostly, Group A, the random Sasquatch. Greys,
the little ones, came later, future folklore, Fey.
The other brethren bred, fed, taught us temples, halls
of glory, storied heaven breaking loose this earthly curtain.

IV.

Of glory, story, all hoary heaven broken loose. . . .
Of earthen curtain rent by uncommon comet,
heaven-sent, sing. Of days darkened, deluge,
scab-black blood darkening doors, cicadas, sacrament,
spoor. . . . Of an age archon-addled, the idioms,
all of them, speak. Pharaoh and his fundamental
heart, Moses' mitosis, Joshua high on Gibeon. . . .
Myths make miracle what the sky calls accidental.

Indeed, about celestial visitation
they were never wrong, the old Masters. It's just
they couldn't tell prophecy from planet palpitation,
Yahweh from the yaw of interstellar wanderlust.
The comet that bought the Hebrews free from scarab
toasted, too, the armies of Sennacherib.

V.

Toasted, the armies of Sennacherib laid
down their lives lying drunk beneath the moon.
Not negligence, not some dusty desert deity,
but love, the goddess of love grown large, stayed
their hearts, evidence of Venus' second passage
careering through our cosmic cluster. The age
demanded an image, so Jupiter, sprung
clockspring offspring, coughed one up, obligingly.

Venus, comet *fakir*, disburser of manna,
gateway through both red and starry sea, eclipse-
bringer, earth-stopper, harbinger of Hosanna—
it left is mark on Gita, Sura, Torah
with coma, with perilous period. Its ellipse . . .
well, all bodies cycle down. Like sharks. Like ships.

VI.

All bodies cycle down. Like sharks, like a ship's
slow descent into leviathan's soft underbelly,
our neighbors, sentient or no, have settled
here, kicked up dust, ruckus, religion.
The treasures they have left on sea floor
(our floor, their ceiling) have left us embattled
though, ragged, reluctant to reason. The origin
of the Qa'aba stone, say, or Phaëthon's flaming trip,

the mooned, helmeted heads of Mayan mortuary
art—one wonders which is whose. Ours? Theirs?
When I look up at night, imagining some door
opening between the opening between stares,
I wonder what *they* see in us. Have they, too, mistaken
the matter of the murky deep for Jenny Hanivers, kraken?

VII.

The matter of the murky deep. Jenny Hanivers.
Kraken. The problem with belief is its root
in the forsaken. Proof, by definition, withers
the soul's necessary suspicion. So the mute
accusation of the stars, the greater body
of alien bodies we've known to be among
us must remain remains only. Each shoddy
assembly of facts, gods, Freudian faux pas

may leave much of the galaxial song unsung,
yet strangely the strain is never more clear than when
that great gaping lack smacks us with its loss
of *being* loss, becomes a presence, lung
for those who cannot breathe, but wholly, space.
Those who must, in course, reclaim communion.

The Astronomer

For we are the local embodiment of the Cosmos grown
to self-awareness. We have begun to contemplate our
origins: starstuff pondering the stars . . .

—Carl Sagan

I.

With the odd, with emanations, with each
dowried ion begotten by marriage (arranged
or no) between ourselves and the out of reach
rose-tinted stars from which we've been estranged,
with stertorous sons of stellar nurseries,
Cepheids whose breathing we gauge our own age by,
with so many singular singularities,
useful, universal dignitaries to dissect, why

little grey men? Trust me, intelligence
will rout us out, teach us insignificance,
show us something about intransigence.
But until that then, until when has been,
it's all about knowing the difference between
the sought after seeing, the seeming, the seen.

II.

The sought after—seeing this seeming green
and pale blue dot—the extraterrestrial eye
some dream to be aware, out there, awake . . .
what possible predilection could it glean
from casting our direction? Why, for the sake
of those who haven't, exactly, clues, why
choose this world? There are only two dead
giveaways something other than plankton

might be breeding here, seething over red
embankments of life-like clay, only to crank one
hovel out after another: the scrimmage
line of stone, that great snake-like grave of slave
bone China calls a wall; this, and cattle farts. Save
these, we've not a thing to show. So much for image.

III.

We've nothing much to show "them" but the image
of Hitler (our 1936 Olympic games),
six decades of sitcoms, a few bombs, *Mary
Tyler Moore*. Nazis and polyester, then, our
mascots to the stars. It's not that the tenor
won't change, of course; others with higher aims
have already sent, say, Beethoven packing.
And naked bodies, ours, wander the only freeway

left picketed with what the earth is lacking,
an absence of signs. But later—in our dotage,
after all those dull, dry years it will have to take
our waves to find a shore on which to break—
should some alien answer's hour roll round at last,
will we be ashamed of what we've asked?

IV.

Will we be ashamed of what we've asked?
Perhaps the better question is what sort
of ears might hear. And more: what's to say
their Sagan there must have them? The vast
ballast we carry, that ribonucleic record
of four billion years spent learning how to stay
erect, the binocular bias of a species
weaned on photosynthesis and feces,

all our preconceptions of conception,
natural selection, histories built on rude
restlessness, agrarian resurrection
myth, sexual repression, food, crude
culinary taboo, all intrude, force us to conclude
(we turf toughs of star stuff) a proud perfection.

V.

The real turf toughs of star stuff, the proud
perfection our cosmosphere *aux* biosphere
has been fine-tuning itself for, may not be
us. Imagine interstellar intelligence
of protoplasmic cloud; harmonic resonance
so complex it's self-aware; busy
wormhole worker bees riddling the now, the here
in imitation of jumped-up primate brachiation;

a casteless, chlorophyllic civilization
whose heliotropic cities, bowed
between their own globe and globby night,
reproduce by discharge—each village, clan,
spent like sweetgum spoor bent on cosmic flight.
Now try to imagine such species care, or give a techno-damn.

VI.

Trying to imagine such species would care one
whit, would give a tinker's damn for what they may
not even recognize as life seems to miss
the point. The way to understanding lies
not along the shortest forest path: their coming,
or *having* come already. No, the barren
conclusions many still cling to like Luciferan
locks, the assumption our location is *tres*

important neglects the real wonder of being
able to wonder at all. Both pull us to the center
of ourselves where, Dante might venture,
Satan himself worries our worst thirsts, our yens,
from scratch. But, in knowing longing, first we must descend,
circle by circle cycling down the long way to the end.

VII.

Circle by circle, cycling down, the long way nears
its end. Each rock-pocked rockpile robots maneuver,
each rocket-picked planetary pocket emptied of "sin,"
ceases to astound with silence, yet appears
all the more to confound, no longer a louver
between us and the next last light. Really, then,
the skies we navigate today, the spiny
shoals of night's atolls, limpet-lit, briny,

all Chthonic waters we suppose to never close, won't.
Ceaselessly, we are born back up into the down
of where there is no down but sun and stone,
the stony, Sol-strewn detritus of moon. One
child of gravity follows, always, others from the font;
with the odd, with awe's creation, knows reunion.

The Colonel

When I'm a veteran with only one eye
I shall do nothing but look at the sky.

—W. H. Auden

I.

In the sky once (twice, some say) night opened
up enough for us to read its entrails.
Me, I'm not so sure that I'm not sure they're right
anymore. I used to know planes by contrails
only, military (read Navy) etiquette,
a few good men who knew the difference
between fact and fancy. But some things so offend
the mind, it relieves you of command, leaves you

wondering, why here? Why now? Why fiddle
for cat, dish for spoon? At times the evidence
seems paltry, desultory, poetic piddle
in a vast, pedantic pool of nonsense, but, Blue
Book or no, the days remain I lie in bed,
visions of visitation dancing in my head.

II.

Visions of visitation dancing in my head,
I loop the scene beneath each lid-locked veil,
each caul I call an eye, then, like some vaguely
human rotoscope, flip images till they're dead
again. Five Avengers left Ft. Lauderdale
that day to the tune of clear skies, a pseudo-sortie
made up of men already in league with the sea.
What no one knew was out there, that pale

horse even old Ichabod ran from, must have led
them a merry chase. At just past half past three,
the radio caught them, their madness, mid-travail.
Whatever happened, happened in the dead
air between halo and horror, horror and haunted wood.
"Even the ocean doesn't look as it should. . . ."

III.

Even the ocean doesn't look as it should
anymore. Those men in my command, the fifteen
flyers of Flight 19, vanished like Dali's blue
dog in "The Inventions of the Monsters." How could
he have known his experimental pigment, that new
crucible, would show, only, in having *been*?
It is, I suppose, the nature of art to confront
that terrible titillation of being misread,

but what does disappearance, a hunt for the hunt
itself, mean? Perhaps loss—the familiar shiver
like that which moves us, mindless, to mind red
lights—is all. Certainly, it isn't the clever
organization of lenses that stops us dead.
Maybe absence, essence, the presence of dread.

IV.

Maybe absence, essence, the presence of some
dread we could not have trained them for spirited
them away. The same vast latticework of lack
formed from native-named street signs, states, bric-a-brac—
that which holds me here enthralled by what's riveted
to seems—must have unpieced the humdrum
peace of their normal, slightly northward tack
and turned them back into themselves, toward

what—pilot or colonel, knock-kneed schoolmaster
or dead Delaware—everyone shuns. . . .
Not UFOs, necessarily, but the bones
of the matter: the fear that when we ford
the water, unmerciful disaster
will loom from foam, from formlessness, from aster.

V.

Risk must form from foam, from formlessness,
from each bare-assed stir stirred up by dips
taken in the deep. What captain never trips
over the very sky he has undertaken
to strip the mystery from? What harness
that bites the lip, chafes the temple, is not mistaken
for better means to guide the ride toward home?
When Lt. Taylor ceded his command to Stiver,

when one said, ". . . looks like we're entering white water,"
and St. Elmo's bogey, ungainly as a raven, croaked
their way clear to return to salty loam,
one of them, at least one lost, limned soul
must have, cracking up, cracked at last, *We're fucked*,
just before something holy filled the whole.

VI.

Just before something holy filled the whole
cabin window, right after the radio clammed
shut. . . . These moments helm the headlessness
that haunts me. So they vanished, so what? Damned
or only dreaming beneath polydactyl caress;
felled or held in stasis in the fold
of a Capellan carrier bay; harpists
or hybrid harpies kept alive in genes

of bug-eyed, bastard offspring. . . . Regardless,
it's the guard at the gate of diminishing
returns that gets me. The more I try to glean
the way it must have been, the less frightening
seem the sodden yaws that draw me. Sirens. Beetling rocks.
Davy Jones' private pox, that untooled, tenanted, tri-cornered box.

VII.

Davy Jones, primate locks, a love of the untooled,
tenanted, tri-cornered box the sea which claims
how all that's human *isn't*, yet human remains,
all loss, all dross, all the sacrificially unschooled,
wife, country, duty, every awed honor,
daughter, son, adopted soldier, Donner
Pass, *gravitas*, the way we run this regimen of days,
the ceding of our second sight to haze,

everything we now consider fable fodder, epic,
the hera's apotheosis, the epileptic
become prophet, messiah, pariah again,
Mozart, *Middangeard*, *maya*, Chopin. . . .
It's a sea-change we're in for, for more than fifteen men,
if in the sky (once, twice some say) indeed night opened.

The Magician

That grinning, glowing, globular invader of your living
room is an inhabitant of the pumpkin patch, and if your
doorbell rings and nobody's there, that was no Martian . . .
it's Halloween.

—Orson Welles

I.

Its else, to them, lets logic spill through. Upend,
suspend what they no longer want to be real,
return them to credulity and they'll shill
the very silk from their souls to keep "prudent" pretend.
I knew this from, perhaps, five. Before
radio, before film, before even inconsequence,
I was drawn to it, magic, that boyish lore
conjured into career. When, then, did I chance

to peak, Iowa? There are signs, always, one should doubt
one's own tales, the blunderbuss trussed up as history.
Yes, I tramped the world at twelve, could count
the Bard a shard in my repertoire a good while
before that, graced the stage at three, knew Houdini
even, but nothing charmed charms for long, not gaud, not
    Grover's Mill.

II.

Nothing charmed stays charmed for long, not God,
not Grover's Mill. But when the audience
wants little green men, the film of the century,
an aunt who bathes in Perrier only to disappear
one Sunday in a rickshaw in China,
when they beg for a genius, misunderstood
of course, slugging his way through poverty
hawking cheap wine, when the hag-massed conscience

of the country demands the odd, you nod,
smile, trick up your sleeve and give it the good
Tinsel Town try. Not that Vaudeville ranks minor
billing on the tally sheet of the Grand Exchequer. . . .
It's just that, well, each stage we've built stands for *having* stood;
there's no more holy in holly than promises in wood.

III.

There's no more holy in holly than there's promise
in the sky. I knew this that Halloween,
knew the last best hoax was my own faith
in nothing, but still the sky fell for the poor
rubes who would have bought whatever precipice,
bridgeless, I sold them. I took them in their green
years, hobbled them with hope, fed them the wraith
they were already ready to swallow. *Bore*

no one. Like lightning, that maxim led me,
all fire, fume, forked finesse, into each
irradiated rec-room, from boondocks to beach.
And there, they dangled for me, plunged to the sea.
Philco or fife, magic or Martian or holy shroud. . . .
Lord! Blackstone, Barnum, they would've been proud.

IV.

Lord Blackstone, old Barnum, both would've been proud.
There was that woman, poison in hand, they found
locked in her bathroom, her children huddled
in the tub. "They're coming," was all the muddled
confession they could wring from her. Gas, hunger, death
lobbed by tripod heatray, the threat of each new breath
breathed beneath some suppurating Martian thumb. . . .
Hundreds fled the cities believing the end had come.

Switchboards caught fire, the streets swarmed, police collected
in night's crotch to clutch at what they once protected,
blue ticks worrying a dog worrying his long dead
master's thigh. They clamored for treats, receipts for dread
that no one—Hirohito, Hitler—had the balls yet to redeem.
Magicians know at least this trick: Sustain the waking dream.

V.

Magicians. Know. Least. Each word a trick
to sustain, a waking dream that, once silent,
became radio, movies, me. See, I could
never keep my own trap shut. So I took some
of the fallen with me, so what? It's not
as if I'd knotted the *not* myself around
each pale fruit, each mottled neck just to see
how some sad sap troped his rope's end. No, the kick

I got, I got from what they all thought was meant
for them only. Yes, I provided gopher wood
and hammer, hope, apocalyptic yammer. Dumb
beasts, we always believe we'll leave behind our lot.
Truth is, no matter if we hang, drown, flee,
*some*one's box awaits us, always, false wall down.

VI.

Someone's box awaits us, always, false wall down.
Divided by boards, sometimes swords, mirrors,
compartments within compartments, secret
hollows behind a screen, the smoke between
us and everything else that clearly *isn't*
keeps our demons baying and at bay. Horrors,
bullroarers, God's command to leave for Nineveh,
Jack O'Lanterns, the will of each wisp, swamp gas,

crabgrass, Barnum's termited giant, Piltdown
Man, combustible bushes. . . . Pumpkins remain
pumpkins, no matter how we slice them. *Ask
for fear and unto you it shall be*— Given
this, this frenzy, envy, obsession to be awed,
is it any wonder what we've sought, this box, this sod?

VII.

Is it any wonder that we've sought to box
our God between reels, that we've looked for each
next-best messiah in the dark? No director,
no writer worth a damn ever let that urge
rest. Give a guy the world's largest Erector
Set and, if he owns to that smirch of demiurge
born in the blood, he's got no choice. Reach.
We all want rabbits, hats. We plunge our arms

deep into that deep to steal the little
of Leviathan we dare, borrowing what rocks
faith founders on to build our house of charms—
theater, we call it, show—and here, each rosed bud
promises garden, Havvah even, precious metal
of all else, letting logic spill through, unopened.

The Writer

. . . and since they knew nothing about his life
they lied till they produced another one . . .

—Rainer Maria Rilke

I.

The rhetoric of *no* must begin with union.
In '76 the *whole* union had grown obsessed
with the repressed, with who it was, its own
unknown, mortality, future, what had passed
once for belief in nothing. Now, everything
was up for grabs. Tutankhamun, pyramid
power, Bigfoot, crystal skulls said to sing,
abduction, transmigration, Bermuda's horned grid.

No ship parts, no star charts, no mere rumors
of metal found off the Keys was, well, useless
to us. No. No wonder I grew up saying yes,
collecting each occult inkling, twinkling horror
I could find. From Poe's pit to UFO kit to belly to whale . . .
the assumption always was that I would fail.

II.

The assumption always was that I would fail,
made only as I was for myths and monsters.
I could cobble whole summers from black and white
horrors, old films, old books, fantasies of having
at last a real basement. Each fear a careful
orchestration, each shudder sure but flat
as Lugosi, Chaney, Karloff, the dumpster-
fulls of trading cards plucked from bread wrapping

or ads for glowing, plastic phantoms. The real
fears—My Lai, hippies, cherry bombs blowing
the hands off other children—were hucksters
selling my mother vacant deeds to vacant lots.
She tried to shake me, sugared, from her image of the age
while Daddy snuck me *Eerie Tales* between each Casper's page.

III.

My father's snuck-in *Eerie Tales* I gleaned
for vespers, for understanding of the dark
that dangled above me every time I crawled,
small but vast with questions, into the back
window of my family's Ford Torino
where my sisters packed the nooks and cracks
with blanket. There, I rifled the folio
that mattered, the sky that spun out spark-

full and sprocket-lost above the sprawled
Oklahoma roads we traveled. There, I weaned
myself on jaunts to Ganymede, stellar hive,
and Pleiades. See, I knew only enough
about light to believe my own almost snuffed.
I wanted to be rescued, even then, from everything relative.

IV.

I wanted to be rescued, even then, from everything.
So, relative or no, uncannily, my family framed me
for questioning: For whom did Cain found a city?
If indeed God conceived a lesser light to rule
the night, why, on reflection, isn't it? If even spool
worms ranked passage on Noah's dinghy, what pity
left the Lord long enough to leave the Serengeti's
finest behind? Down the long ice, what amazing

lack of grace granted Neanderthals hope
in an afterlife they'd never see? What pressed
them into pressing flowers into palms
whose loss of grasp they must have guessed
at, pondered, lingered over enough to still grope
for in the dark? Why paint the dead—bound, red—
     like loose-leaf psalms?

V.

In the dark, why paint what's dead? Why bind what's loose? Leaf
through Psalms, Leviticus, Acts? Why prey
on revelation? My own unseasoned taste
for the miraculous drove me to bones
and halos—the cursed, unearthed, unearthly—
'til all I knew revolved around two tombs,
one below, one above: bug-eyed Cro-Magnons
back but dead beside bug-eyed coelacanths, past

unshed; these, and bug-eyed aliens overhead.
I made little distinction between dooms.
They all appalled equally. I guess I feared belief,
feared, yet sought it faithfully in every dread.
Lack too, black like eclipse. I feared the crypt's corona.
I wanted to be Jacob, but was jonesed with Jonah.

VI.

I wanted to be Jacob, but, jonesed with Jonah,
I couldn't give up the fairy tales. Evidence
aside, I still believed an easy Eden.
It must have been the archeology of trees—
a summer spent searching for the barely hidden
doors to glory I never found—that let science
at last resettle my heart. Bread and Torah. . . .
We can live on these alone if we think knees

our only answer to confusion, but as both runner
and wrestler, I found other options in the crouch.
Jonah, attempting to flee the necessary
beating, in looking for some place sunnier,
a getaway from God, gave up. But Jacob, no slouch
in giving back what licks he learned to earn to love, let fly.

VII.

In giving back what licks I learned to earn,
in loving, in letting fly, in letting go,
in calling the infinite out for a belly brawl,
busting God's chops before knuckling under,
calling Her names, biting His ear, denying
Them a single scrap of sand on which to burn
Their bushes or kindle new stars we won't know
for a billion more years, in struggle, that long crawl

to the edge of what I'll never understand, never sunder,
on the vast crest of swoon, in faith, in denying
faith, in confusion, in confronting the irresolute
quark shell *cum* truth, beauty, Bigfoot maybe, that one
God who is my garden can be found: felled fruit,
rhetoric, the *no, although*. . . . Slow resin of reunion.

The Believer

*Two possibilities exist: either we are alone
in the universe or we are not. Both are
equally terrifying.*

—Arthur C. Clarke

I.

Even trusting Augustine's shade, religion
cannot save me from the sky. Faith got me
here. Now, how should it take me away? Up
again, into that sick rose heaven made
of itself the night seven stars invaded
my sleep, my bedroom, me? No. No ship,
no chariot, only a light tunneling into the free
radicals of blood, *my* blood, spine, unspun

gold. . . . Then . . . fragments. Commandments like fires. A faint
urge to name them, label them, force them to stamp feet
so deep into heaven's spinning floor they'd unsaint
me, have to, halved now, grown incomplete
as dreams. Visitations are always incomplete—
elfin, brazen, bawdy, smelling of copper, myrrh, wheat.

II.

Elfin, brazen, bodies smelling of copper,
more wheat penny than hay, they . . . it . . . they . . .
alien ideas of "other" snatched me from what
little life I had and made me less
than afraid. *Fear not.* I kept saying this
is not happening, this is nothing but
high lobe lability, night terrors, womb
memory, a bit of underdone lust,

but the moment, brilliant as Polaris,
rapt me in adamantine, and Caucasus
called me home. When I came to, the tomb
I found myself in seemed solid as seawater,
fraying, about to fray, an uncertain curtain, passionless
play, hole in my soul, stitch in the side of the day.

III.

The whole of that sole, stretched, sidereal day
among stars only understood as angels
I spent remembering how once I'd walked
among the naked statues of Pompeii, talked
to gods there, ones even prostitutes—all bangles,
penis-reliefed sandals—followed. I traced
trails their feet had engraved with erections,
with the words, *Follow me*. I thought how "erased"

must mean something very different to Atlanteans,
to those who never return from the volcano
untouched, every woman abruptly taken
to the precipice of herself, forced to look back, Lo,
into the face of whatever master has mistaken
sacrifice for submission. Then I turned to them, to pray.

IV.

Sacrificing submission, I turned to *them* to pray,
to ask, to mask each fetal face in tomorrow's
nimble nimbus of forget. As if in answer,
they walled me in their tomb, uterine, strobing
in and out of my mind, asking me, *Woman,
why weepest thou?* And again I imagined
them demons, powers, a crude crowd come to Christ
in testament of their lack. They said, *This*

woman was taken up, away from us. She's sinned.
And the light which was also skin, every man
and woman of him, bent down, began probing
the ground, spelling something, some word—cancer
perhaps, fools, rapture—and said, *Get a life.* They rose
then, left me alone, written on, grown unaccountably gay.

V.

Left alone, written on, grown unaccountably gay,
I began to teach, preach to all those lost
who can't seem to accept alternative means
of transport. I gave others reason to believe
their many assumptions, discovered
also I wasn't alone, possessed as I was
with conception. Pregnant, confused, uncovered
at last, I found comfort worrying my past—Bast

the cat, Tiamat the sea, Parvati, Rhea,
Mboze—sufferers, daughters, each of us Eve,
keepers of the chalice, God's clitoris, this
rolling wet nubbin, matter, whose greens
and blues unfold between what folds surround
the shadow of old longing and the final crown.

VI.

In the shadow of old longing, the final crown
crowns amidships, between lips where, bartering
what we bear for an uroboric glory
called retrospect, the Word arrives. Here,
in this world, it's all about bearing, bearing
down, bearing up, giving the self over
to what must never take us away from being
taken up. Assumptions are like peeing

on the brain, our aliens relieving themselves forever
from the future, but *some*thing else must come. Hearing
the footsteps, we shouldn't hide. No musty cellar
then. There's been quite enough of that old story.
No, *I* will tell my child it's only starting.
The genius of the sea is that it's always upside down.

VII.

The genius of the sea is that it's always
upside down, the greater portion of its life
spent treading darkness. Who, then, are we—hive-
bound, Hubble-hobbled, shuttle-cocky—to praise
only those who shaped Angkor Wat's fractal face,
to laud the baobab, koi, ichneumonidae that survive
by digesting comatose caterpillar hosts alive?
What arrogance to think it solely DNA's

role to unpuzzle, perhaps at last rescind,
the anxiety fifty billion galaxies must imply. When
those great glowing prayer wheels descend again,
when they come suckling for me like all God's children
drawn down from the deep, I will go, cold, without question,
even trusting. It's a fusty blade, religion.

We all must greet it, fleshless, in the end.

THE HEAT DEATH
OF THE UNIVERSE

*And where we had thought to find an abomination
we shall find a god; where we had thought
to slay another, we shall slay ourselves . . .*

—Joseph Campbell

The Heat Death
of the Universe

It was like catching your God with Her knickers
down. I found out one day the universe must
end. Fourth grade, back of the class where books
lined the walls with all the words I'd ever need.
There, between gloss and cardboard, cardboard
and crayon marginalia, I discovered
what I'd been taught to fear. Something very like
a coelacanth, a fish, Mr. Limpet
with feet, peddling up bog banks to test
the air. Blasphemy. And worse—Baptist
that I was—the rest of the story. What
came before, what must, according to Bohr,
inevitably follow. The birth of atom,
the death of atom's children. A fuller version
of creation than I'd known, been
allowed. Revelation without apocalypse,
apocalypse without demons (Maxwell
notwithstanding). It was all there, tritone,
nearly 3-D, all I could ever ask for
in a doomsday scenario. The heat death
of everything, the cold slowing of heaven's
hurled bodies, the gradual extinction
of what seemed would expand forever.
Funny, but Fenrir never struck me
like this, that quaint Nordic myth of how
it all might end in snow—slow, zero-laden
stasis. The great wolf presiding over
what couldn't last with his last blast of feral
breath, his great howl, growl by growl growing
silent as ice between here and the end
of the world. But *this*. This was dangerous.

It claimed a kind of authority, say, the story
of those five Chinese brothers didn't. So I did
what I had to do. Approached the teacher, Woods,
Mrs. Woods. Showed her the book. Asked her
to burn it, hide it, take it as far away
from me and my faith as her own faith
in me would allow. Coolidge Elementary.
When the days wind down and the sun begins
at last to consume what it has given, I
wonder, still, if that book will remain. There.
Top shelf. Too high for me to reach. Beached.
Unburned. Burning with all its answers.